How to Get Out of an Abusive Relationship

An Essential Step-by-Step Guide for Identifying the Signs of an Abusive Relationship, and Leaving It for a Brighter Future

by Bernie Cotterill

Table of Contents

Introduction 1

Chapter 1: How to Identify the Signs of an Abusive Relationship 7

Chapter 2: Constructing a Rock-Solid Support System 19

Chapter 3: Planning and Implementing Your Exit .. 27

Chapter 4: How to Overcome Thoughts of Staying. 31

Chapter 5: Beginning Your New Life 35

Conclusion 39

Introduction

To anybody looking in from the outside, getting out of an abusive relationship may appear to be as easy as packing up and leaving. If you have personally been a victim of an abusive partner's behavior, however, you will know that the reality of getting out of an abusive relationship poses a much more complex challenge.

Depending on a number of factors, such as your living arrangement, your financial setup, and perhaps even an ominously looming threat to your safety or physical wellbeing, even the mere idea of leaving will undoubtedly be fraught with frustration, an element of fear, and some genuine cause for concern. It's never easy making a big decision such as moving on from a relationship, especially an abusive one, even though you've clearly identified the need to do so. However difficult it may seem, the inevitability of the situation is that in order to realize the potential of the brighter future that's lying in wait for you, the very bold decision to move on simply has to be made.

Abuse in a relationship can rear its ugly head in a number of different forms, and at times, you may not even be sure of whether you're truly in an abusive relationship or not. When the abuse you're suffering from in your relationship is clearly distinguishable, your need to escape will become much more apparent.

Whether you're experiencing the physical, emotional, or verbal abuse yourself or it's someone you care about who's stuck in an abusive relationship, read on to be provided with a solid plan of action to break the cycle, make a clean getaway, and move on with your new life.

With a determined attitude and clear guidance, the cycle of abuse will finally come to an end. In this book, you will learn how to identify the signs of abuse, how to construct a rock-solid support structure, when and how to implement your exit plan, and how to stick to your decision and begin a new life. If you're ready to experience the bright, positive future that awaits you, let's get started!

© Copyright 2015 by Miafn LLC - All rights reserved.

This document is geared towards providing reliable information in regards to the topic and issue covered. The publication is sold with the idea that the publisher is not required to render accounting, officially permitted, or otherwise, qualified services. If advice is necessary, legal or professional, a practiced individual in the profession should be ordered.

- From a Declaration of Principles which was accepted and approved equally by a Committee of the American Bar Association and a Committee of Publishers and Associations.

In no way is it legal to reproduce, duplicate, or transmit any part of this document in either electronic means or in printed format. Recording of this publication is strictly prohibited and any storage of this document is not allowed unless with written permission from the publisher. All rights reserved.

The information provided herein is stated to be truthful and consistent, in that any liability, in terms of inattention or otherwise, by any usage or abuse of any policies, processes, or directions contained within is solely and completely the responsibility of the recipient reader. Under no circumstances will any legal responsibility or blame be held against the publisher for any reparation, damages, or monetary loss due to the information herein, either directly or indirectly.

Respective authors own all copyrights not held by the publisher.

The information herein is offered for informational purposes solely, and is universal as so. The presentation of the information is without contract or any type of guarantee assurance.

The trademarks that are used are without any consent, and the publication of the trademark is without permission or backing by the trademark owner. All trademarks and brands within this book are for clarifying purposes only and are the owned by the owners themselves, not affiliated with this document.

Chapter 1: How to Identify the Signs of an Abusive Relationship

It's worth emphasizing that identifying whether you're in an abusive relationship or not isn't always a simple process. This is especially true if you're right in the middle of an unhappy relationship in which the blurred lines between abuse and other sources of your unhappiness exist at every turn. Dealing with the reality of an unhappy relationship is often a great source of some serious confusion, even if at times you may feel as if you're to blame.

When you try to blame yourself for your partner's abusive actions you obviously already are in an abusive relationship and probably know it, but there are many more signs you can look out for to help you determine exactly what an abusive relationship encompasses. You should never blame yourself for someone else's abusive behavior. No matter what you may or may not have done, and no matter how sour the relationship has turned out, there is never any justification for one person to abuse another, in any way.

What exactly is abuse and more specifically, what exactly is an abusive relationship?

Since people are different in numerous ways, one person's perception of abuse may differ slightly to another person's, so the finer details of defining abuse will ultimately come down to you as an individual. On a broader scale though, abuse is when you are deliberately made to experience ill-treatment—when your partner deliberately treats you badly in one or more of a number of different ways, including physical, sexual or even emotional ill-treatment. Some examples of abuse in its various guises can include experiences of your partner's deliberate efforts to try and control your behavior, threatening you with violence, hurling insults at you, humiliating you in public, making you feel scared, getting overly jealous, and even belittling you in any way. Abuse doesn't always only encompass ill-treatment aimed directly at you and can also take the form of your partner threatening your loved-ones with violence, or threatening your possessions with malicious intent to cause physical damage.

Your partner may even be abusing you financially, through something like deliberately withholding your pre-agreed upon access to funds that you need for your basic livelihood. If there is a child involved, abuse could even go as far as taking the form of your partner trying to turn the child against you.

In short, any experience of deliberate ill-treatment from your partner constitutes abuse and you'll generally know that you're being abused if you are unduly made to feel extreme physical or emotional discomfort.

It's very important to be able to make a distinction between something like a lover's quarrel and an abusive relationship. As with any healthy relationship, you will have fights (none of which should ever get physical) and you will argue. At times you may even have heated and passionate arguments, but knowing where the line between arguing/fighting and abuse is comes down to your ability to identify the cardinal signs of an abusive relationship. These cardinal signs of an abusive relationship can be fundamentally grouped into five categories, including:

- Physical Violence & Sexual Assault
- Threats
- Belittlement
- Possessiveness
- Excessive and Unreasonable Jealousy

Physical Violence & Sexual Assault

Perhaps the most easily identifiable form of abuse is physical abuse, but by no means does this mean that this is the only form of abuse in existence or, in fact, the worst form of abuse. Any form of abuse can make life a living hell for you as the victim, but physical abuse leaves you in physical pain and discomfort. Extreme cases of physical abuse in a relationship take the form of your partner beating you or hurting you, but if your partner shoves you, grabs you, pushes you around or even harms your family members and pets, that also constitutes physical abuse.

Similarly, sexual assault as a form of physical abuse doesn't necessarily only constitute extreme cases such as intra-relationship rape, but if your partner is forcing you to have sex or engage in sexual acts you don't want to engage in, that's also a form of sexual abuse.

If you find yourself experiencing physical pain or extreme discomfort as a result of the deliberate actions of your partner, you can consider yourself to be in a physically abusive relationship.

Threats

Although physical abuse in a relationship most visibly displays signs of the abuse, emotional abuse in its various forms can be just as disheartening if not more destructive to your well-being. If you're constantly made to live out your life in fear of what your partner threatens to do, consider yourself the victim of a form of emotional abuse. If your partner threatens you with violence, threatens your loved ones with violence, shouts at you and threatens to deliberately break some of your possessions of value, this is a form of emotional abuse.

If somebody claims to love somebody else, or at least claims to care about somebody else, the last thing he or she would want to do is deliberately instill any form of fear in the other person. If your partner truly loved you or cared about you, you would actually be made to feel safe in whatever way possible. It's important for you to understand this because the worst of threats could very easily escalate into a threatened action actually being carried-out, often with dire consequences. It's also not at all good to have to constantly live in fear of some harm befalling you should your partner go all the way next time and actually carry out the threats. You don't want to find yourself physically harmed to such an extent that the damage is permanent, or even fatal, to you, your loved-ones, or even your possessions or livelihood.

Sadly, having to endure threats makes for one of the most tolerated forms of emotional abuse people put up with and constantly let slide. They are misguided by the fallacy that since their partners haven't as yet carried out the abusive actions they threaten them with, these threats don't in themselves constitute abuse.

Do not take your partner's threats lightly. Being threatened is very much a form of abuse in a relationship and it accounts for enough of a reason to want to get out of that abusive relationship. Threats also form part of your partner's efforts to control you and, while every relationship inevitably comes with a measure of sacrifices and compromises, those sacrifices and compromises should be made out of your own free will. The moment you need to be threatened with violence or any other form of abusive action to behave a certain way, it just establishes another reason why you need to move on from such a relationship that is clearly not right for you.

Belittlement

Belittlement is another form of emotional (and verbal) abuse and it entails your partner's deliberate attempts to make you feel bad about yourself. This could include direct insults hurled at you or it can take the form of your partner deliberately putting you down privately or publicly. Remember that it is entirely up to you, and it is your tolerance for your partner's belittlement which ultimately determines whether you construe it as abuse or not. Room for constructive criticism and honesty should always be made in every relationship, but there is a stark contrast between your partner playfully teasing you a bit and maliciously insulting your intelligence, capabilities, looks or mental well-being.

If you find that your opinion of yourself is eroded by your partner's actions, allow yourself to admit to the fact that you are the victim of emotional and verbal abuse in the form of belittlement. This belittlement could even take the form of your partner making you feel as if you don't measure up to some other people you're constantly being compared with, often very unfavorably and unfairly.

It is while enduring belittlement from their partner, when a lot of victims of abusive relationships find ways to blame themselves for the abuse, with that self-blame fire fueled by the partner also putting the blame on them. The abuser often blames you for all the problems you're both facing in the relationship and accepts none of the responsibility. Remember that you are not to blame for your partner's abusive behavior and abuse can never be justified in any way. Make sure you understand that if your partner claims to be able to do much better than you, then he or she should go ahead and leave the relationship to pursue the greener pastures you seemingly don't measure up to. You have the exact same right to your freedom and you should never let yourself believe that belittlement is only a benign form of abuse in a relationship.

Possessiveness

While any caring or loving partner would naturally want to feel as if their feelings of love are reciprocated, you do not want to feel as if somebody else owns you. Possessiveness is another common sign of being in an abusive relationship, with the abuse carried out physically through your partner actively trying to control who you interact with and where you go. In particular, they get angry when you don't comply with their controlling demands.

A good relationship should never feel like a prison sentence in any way and you can very easily identify possessiveness as a form of abuse in a relationship through your partner's efforts to excessively check on you to see exactly where you are, who you're with and what you're up to. In this instance it can be very tricky to distinguish between genuine concern and possessiveness. When you're unsure of whether your partner's efforts are out of genuine concern or if they are a sign of possessiveness, simply evaluate how much freedom you feel you have in the situation. Are your movements restricted in any way, even if by fear of getting your partner angry? Do you constantly feel edgy or jumpy, knowing that the phone is going to ring at any moment, with some direct questions as to your whereabouts and the associated reasons?

If the answer is "yes", then you need to take a closer look at the possibility of being a victim of an abusive relationship, with possessiveness being the indicative factor.

Excessive and Unreasonable Jealousy

Excessive and unreasonable jealousy is very closely related to possessiveness as a sign of being in an abusive relationship. In fact, most excessive and unreasonable jealousy as part of being in an abusive relationship stems from possessiveness, through which your partner harbors feelings of entitlement over you.

If your partner tries to isolate you from your friends and family and wants you all to him/herself, all the time, the relationship very quickly goes from being "in love" to "possessive and jealous." The abuse-factor comes into play when you start to feel as if you are restricted from or forbidden to see your friends and family, even if only to avoid the conflict of a confrontation. You should naturally avoid actions which induce jealousy in your partner, but when you're being accused of things like infidelity or flirting without good reason, it's nothing less than jealousy which forms part of being in an emotionally abusive relationship.

Listen to your gut

The common signs of an abusive relationship detailed above serve as a means through which you can confirm whether you're in an abusive relationship or not, and subsequently whether you need to take steps towards exiting the relationship. Reaching a conclusive perspective can be very difficult, especially amidst the many factors which contribute to your unhappiness in a particular relationship. If you truly have trouble making your mind up however, simply try to identify any genuine experience you've had to endure, as detailed above, which suggests that you're in an abusive relationship.

Don't try to make excuses for your partner, however wonderful the relationship may have been in the past.

If you're wondering whether or not you are in an abusive relationship, at the very least, your gut is letting you know that you are and you need to do something about it.

Chapter 2: Constructing a Rock-Solid Support System

The previous chapter gave you a good grounding as to how to confirm whether you are indeed in an abusive relationship or not. It was necessary to detail some common signs characteristic of abusive relationships, because moving forward, some of the suggested steps you're going to have to take in order to get out are very serious, and some even have serious legal implications.

The next step in the process of leaving your abusive relationship is a very delicate one as it entails your commencement of some actionable stances to be executed or relied upon when making your exit. Perhaps, it also involves the most crucial step because from this point onwards the effects of the next action you take will probably shape your immediate future in a permanent way.

Depending on the severity of the abuse you suffer in your relationship, you are going to choose one or more actions to get going with, as detailed in the next chapter. Before you do that however, you first need to construct a safety net for yourself, in the form of a solid support structure.

Talk to Someone

It is of vital importance that you get someone else involved. Confide in someone you trust and let them know what you're going through. Do not feel ashamed. Yes, it is very hard to have to re-live any abusive experiences through talking about them, but now is not the time for you to feel ashamed, and it is very important that at least one other person knows about what you're going through and what you plan to do about it.

If you're not really comfortable discussing the matter with a loved-one (although this is highly recommended), you can get in touch with a social worker or even join a support group. You'll be very surprised as to exactly how much support is available to you and you may even be surprised as to where that much-needed support comes from. An outsider's point-of-view may even offer you some fresh perspective and perhaps even help you uncover a solution that has been right under your nose all this time.

Depending on the severity of the abuse you suffer, in case something really bad happens, you'll at least have one other reference point to help corroborate your version of events—the true version of events. If you're planning to leave your partner, relay some of the details to your confidant. Tell them exactly when you're going to confront your partner with your decision to leave and perhaps ask them to come along with you to offer support.

When abusive partners are confronted with the knowledge that someone else knows about what's going on in the relationship, they are less likely to do something rash in fear of landing in hot water. Abusive partners are often very needy and they'll most probably try to convince you to re-consider your decision and stay. In this instance, a present third-party could make for that much-needed voice of reason you'll undoubtedly be very prone to ignore, given the confusion understandably induced by the circumstances.

Organize an Emergency Contact

Ideally, you might want to let your former partner know of your decision to leave once you've already left, in which case a simple phone call will do. Naturally though, you might not have enough time to get your things together without being "caught in the act", or you might have to make different living arrangements, such as those which require *the partner* to leave instead of you. If it has to come down to a face-to-face breaking of the news, and possibly a confrontation, make sure you have someone on the alert that you might have to call should things get ugly. This emergency contact could even be the local police or a social worker, but it is important in case of any unplanned eventualities.

<u>Know Your Rights</u>

Depending on the seriousness and progressive evolvement of your relationship, some legal issues may ensue with regards to things like your living arrangements, access to joint financial accounts or even custody of the children, if any children are involved. Make sure to conduct thorough research, but do so with the aid of a qualified professional in the social services field. Often getting in touch with a social worker will help you connect with legal experts whose sole existence is for dealing with cases just like yours. Even if you may not be able to afford legal fees you should relay all of this information to a social worker.

Know Where to Go for Medical Treatment or Counseling

In the case of a physically-abusive relationship, be prepared for any eventuality by knowing exactly where you'd go for medical treatment. Keep the number of a counselor handy as well—you'll need some professional psychological assistance to help you deal with what is undoubtedly a stressful situation.

Organize a Place to Stay

Once you make your break from your abusive relationship, you'll need to have a place to go. As mentioned earlier, the parting of ways between you and your abusive partner may require them to make alternative living arrangements instead of you, so you should have everything planned and organized beforehand. If this is indeed the case (your partner needing to move instead of you), you can almost certainly expect them to employ some delay-tactics and perhaps truthfully claim not to have somewhere to go. In planning for that *you* might even have to make those alternative living arrangements for your partner.

The bottom line is you must have somewhere to stay immediately following your necessary breakup.

These five pointers constitute most the considerations you'll need to construct a post-abusive-relationship safety net, with the final piece of the puzzle being that of your financial well-being. If you already had a job and were independent prior to getting into what has now become an abusive relationship, your financial security is probably already taken care of. If you don't already have a source of income, do everything in your power (with the help of your confidants and other people in your support-structure) to make sure you can find a source of income.

Some of these considerations as part of your safety net and support-structure may appear to be a bit obvious, but in the midst of a messy breakup from an abusive relationship, it can be very hard to think of even the smallest, routine details. Worse yet, if the abuse you endured presented itself in the form of a controlling and possessive partner, it might be a challenge to complete even the simplest of tasks, like applying for a job online.

You can never plan too much as far as your safety net goes, even if it means factoring in considerations such as living in a shelter for a while and temporarily getting by on government grants.

Chapter 3: Planning and Implementing Your Exit

When it comes down to the actual moment of making the breakaway, your approach will be dictated by the circumstances and severity of your abusive relationship.

If you need to escape without the immediate knowledge of your abusive partner, make sure all parties involved are fully aware of the plan of action, right down to the finest details. For example, if there are kids involved, they should be on the alert that a sudden "unplanned" trip may pop up at any time, and be prepared accordingly. Otherwise it can be very difficult to keep things under wraps if you have to discuss it prior to the planned escape.

If you need to escape undetected in this way, you're most likely in a physically abusive relationship and you understandably fear the eruption of your partner's violent behavior in the getaway process.

If putting your goods together is going to raise some eyebrows and fears of the eruption of violence, you can go down to your local police station and request to be escorted by a law enforcement official as you go back for the rest of your possessions. Since your exit in this case will most probably be very swift and perhaps hasty, make sure you know exactly where all your important documents are. Documents such as your IDs, social security cards, marriage license, birth certificates, car and title deeds, and other essentials should be easily located and accessible so that you have everything you'll need for your new life going forward.

Get acquainted with your partner's schedule so that you know exactly when the best moment to get away may be.

Don't make plans to go to a mutual friend as this will open up the door for your former abusive partner to easily gain access to you.

Be sure to collect any evidence of the abuse you suffered as this can make for some solid ground on which to extend legal proceedings, should the need arise. With the law behind you and the subsequent technical expertise. Even deleted messages and other documents can be recovered on your mobile device or on your computer, so if possible, make sure to get away with these items in-tow.

Finally, once the breakup and exit is in effect, let this symbolize a point of no-return. There is no looking back from here on since changing your mind will not only instill self-doubt, but will also cause all parties and authorities involved to doubt the credibility of your claims. Your abusive partner will also not have a complete appreciation of the seriousness of the abuse and all the time and effort put into planning the exit will have been for nothing.

Stick to your guns and when the time comes to leave, make sure you get over the threshold of ending the relationship and actually leaving, whatever happens.

Chapter 4: How to Overcome Thoughts of Staying

Even once you're dead-set on leaving your abusive relationship behind, that small voice inside of you telling you to stay will come to life, and it can be very persuasive. Whatever you do, do not listen to it. Thoughts of staying will be sparked by considerations such as the fact that your partner may perhaps not have been violent all the time, that your partner abuses you because they love you (believe it or not), that things will get better or that the abuse was just a one-off thing.

Perhaps you may be scared of what the future holds for you going forward or you may even be scared of what your former abusive partner will do to get even or try to punish you further for taking a stand. Feelings of the abuse being your own fault are particularly fertile in the heat of the moment, and such feelings may present themselves very strongly at this point.

The best way to overcome any thoughts of staying at this stage is relatively unpleasant and painful, but it is very necessary nonetheless and it entails re-living the abuse you suffered. When you start to feel yourself contemplating whether to stay and you are entertaining thoughts that leaving is bad decision, think back to the worst moments of abuse you experienced and imagine yourself walking right back into that living hell if you turn around and decide to stay.

Re-living the darkest moments of your experienced abuse, is not only guaranteed to work in overcoming any thoughts of you going back, but will also help as part of your healing process. Look straight ahead to a brighter, perhaps more challenging future, but don't entertain any thoughts of going back.

Chapter 5: Beginning Your New Life

While the reality of your life after enduring an abusive relationship may require you to have some sort of contact with your former abusive partner, keep the contact to a minimum and only allow contact where absolutely necessary. If possible, only communicate over the phone or via email, instant messaging, etc.

An example of mandatory contact would be if there are children involved in the separation, or indeed if there are some legal proceedings under way. Perhaps you both need to iron out the logistics of how your joint assets are to be shared or you need to make arrangements for outstanding bills to be paid, children's visitations to be sorted out, etc. In such cases, communication and perhaps contact is unavoidable, but make sure that if communication and contact is necessary, only the business of the day is discussed or taken care of.

Do not let the communication lead to discussions of how your partner has changed and wants a second chance. Sometimes your former abusive partner will try to take advantage of the communication channels to inflict further abuse on you, so don't give them any openings. If your former partner wishes to apologize, that's as far as it goes and no further.

In order to successfully move on with your life after your abusive relationship, the best thing to do is immediately immerse yourself in carving out a better future for yourself. Unless it's part of a professional therapy session, don't dwell on the relationship that was—get going with your new career, or make a meal out of your job-hunting, new hobby or anything else which keeps you busy and symbolizes your new life away from an abusive relationship. At the same time, where possible, cut all ties with your former abusive partner. If you owned a house together for example, make arrangements to sell the house. Inform mutual friends of the new, separate approach to your friendship if such a friendship is really that important to your new life.

In the future—when the time is right—don't be scared to give other love interests a chance, for fear of a repeat of what you just came out of. If anything, you will have come away from your abusive relationship much wiser, armed with a developed ability to spot abusive-partner tendencies well in advance.

Re-connect with friends and family you might have been deprived contact with and go to some of the places you were restricted from under the constraints of your abusive relationship.

Conclusion

Getting out of any relationship is usually already difficult enough, let alone with the complexity added to the process when it's an *abusive* relationship you're attempting to get out of.

Breaking free from an abusive relationship becomes even more difficult when the relationship has evolved and developed to create co-dependency between you and your partner, like if you have children, joint financial accounts or joint property ownership. You might also not even be completely sure of whether you are indeed in an abusive relationship or not, at which juncture it becomes important for you to know exactly how to identify the signs of an abusive relationship.

Physical violence & sexual assault, threats of violence towards you or your loved ones, belittlement, possessiveness, and excessive, unreasonable jealousy are all signs of being in an abusive relationship, which can be categorized into the different forms of abuse, including physical, emotional (verbal) and psychological abuse. Abuse in a relationship can also take the form of financial abuse, but the bottom line is you'll know that you're in an abusive relationship if you are either physically or emotionally ill-treated.

Once you've ascertained that you are indeed in an abusive relationship, the next step entails building up a support structure or safety net to help you cope with your decision to exit the abusive relationship. Do some thorough research on your legal rights, organize an emergency contact, tell someone about your situation and find out where you can get medical and psychological treatment and support. Also, work towards securing your financial future, such as searching for a job or perhaps applying for a social grant in case you're not already employed.

When it comes down to the actual implementation of your exit plan, make sure you're adequately prepared for possible confrontations or a backlash from your abusive partner. You can even get law enforcement officials involved if there is a need for such measures. However the actual event plays out, make sure your stance to leave is as clear as daylight and that you don't entertain any thoughts of changing your mind and perhaps back-tracking. Stick to your decision and look towards your brighter, more challenging but necessary transition into a future without the pain and suffering caused by your former abusive partner.

Try to live in the moment and don't dwell on past experiences any more than is absolutely necessary, in the process severing as many ties with your ex-partner as you possibly can.

Finally, I'd like to thank you for purchasing this book! If you found it helpful, I'd greatly appreciate it if you'd take a moment to leave a review on Amazon. Thank you!